The Big Bo
Pick
and Draw
Activities

Setting kids' imagination free to
explore new heights of learning

MW00823865

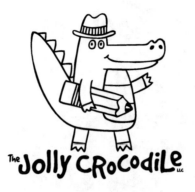

The Jolly Crocodile

The Big Book of Pick and Draw Activities

*Setting kids' imagination free
to explore new heights of learning*

ISBN: 978-0-9883510-0-4

Printed in the United States of America
First Printing 2012

Book design by Lorinda Gray
ragamuffincreative.com

NOTE TO EDUCATORS:

PAD and the Common Core State Standards

THE COMMON CORE STATE STANDARDS (CCSS) have been adopted by 46 states as their education standards. Pick and Draw can support the standards in many ways. For updated information on the standards, see www.corestandards.org.

The CCSS is divided into two levels: the Anchor Standards and the grade level standards. The Anchor Standards lay out what a high school graduate should know and be able to do. The grade level standards express the Anchor Standards in grade-appropriate, developmental and sequential skills for that specific grade.

To provide a correlation of specific skills that the PAD can help teach, it is impossible to discuss every grade level. Instead, we will identify appropriate Anchor Standards. Teachers will need to drill down to the grade level standards to determine specific lesson goals.

Here are some Anchor Standards that may be generally applied to PAD:

READING—There's no reading for PAD, so this doesn't apply.

WRITING—These Anchor Standards will apply when PAD is used as a prewriting strategy or a revision strategy as the students produce a written narrative.

#3. Write narratives to develop real or imagined experiences or events using effective techniques, well-chosen details and well-structured event sequences.

#4. Produce clear and coherent writing in which the development, organization and style are appropriate to the task, purpose and audience.

#5. Develop and strengthen writing as needed by planning, revising, editing, rewriting or trying a new approach.

#10. Write routinely over extended time frames (time for research, reflection and revision) and shorter time frames (a single sitting or a day or two) for a range of tasks, purposes and audiences.

SPEAKING AND LISTENING—These Anchor Standards will apply to the PAD lessons in general as students listen to instructions, work and collaborate on projects and produce presentations based on the PAD work. Of course, the PAD work adds to a student's skills in creating visual displays.

#1. Prepare for and participate effectively in a range of conversations and collaborations with diverse partners, building on others' ideas and expressing their own clearly and persuasively.

#5. Make strategic use of the digital media and visual displays of data to express information and enhance understanding of presentations.

foreword

Universally, kids are thrilled when someone says, "LET'S DRAW!"

EVEN IF YOU'RE NOT AN ART TEACHER, I am thrilled to bring you a simple tool, Pick and Draw card game, to make this happen. In this book you will find fun, hands-on activities to help you use PAD with kids. You will see doors unlock, ideas flourish and confidence grow.

PHOTO BY DANIEL DAVIS 2009

My name is Rich Davis, and I am the inventor of this simple drawing game. For four years I have watched kids and adults enjoy being creative and learn to draw better while using Pick and Draw. It is a phenomenon that

6

continues to unfold even where English is not spoken. Teachers, parents and creative people around the world tell me that it works.

I am a children's book illustrator as well as a teaching artist, and it is my privilege to draw with thousands of kids each year and watch their extraordinary, God-given creativity. Through this simple game, the kids' creativity flows out easily and liberally, unlocking many doors in learning and relationships. It has been amazing to watch.

In this book, I have compiled Pick and Draw activities that other professionals have already used effectively with children. Each chapter is written by a professional in a field related to children and their education. Their expertise and experience will make PAD even more effective as you play the simple game with your students.

As you engage your kids with these fun activities, please take the liberty of making changes where needed in order to suit your own goals.

Simple and fun is always a winning combination!

Rich Davis
Northwest Arkansas, 2012
www.pickanddraw.com

TABLE of CONTENTS

TABLE OF CONTENTS

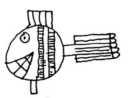

Using Pick and Draw to Teach Talking, Drawing and Writing

overview

WRITING IS FOUNDED on the young child's growing ability to construct images of the world and to communicate those images through diverse forms of media. Young children begin with a piece of paper that is a wide-open space for drawing and progress developmentally from drawing to writing. The following activities are designed to be completed through whole-group lessons, in small groups or during center rotations.

With each one, use Pick and Draw to get students focused on talking, drawing and writing with greater detail, especially related to emotions.

Background

USING THE standard instructions, use the Pick and Draw game in small groups to introduce students to different facial features and expressions. As skill grows, students can move forward to drawing with greater detail and showing their feelings in their drawings and writing. As their skill continues to grow, extend the activity to class book pages, self-portraits and responses to literature.

WHEN FIRST PLAYING the game, young children will have a difficult time filling in the space of their paper and erasing the pencil lines they no longer need. To focus their efforts, begin with 5½"x4¼" squares of paper and small groups with immediate feedback, moving gradually to larger paper and independent work.

As you play the game with students, talk with them about strong feeling words and how the different faces they are creating with the Pick and Draw game illustrate some of those feelings. Move toward more detail as the lessons progress.

Students need substantial talk time to share their thoughts and to verbalize their thinking. The ability to talk and think aloud is an important step in the drawing and writing process because it invites children to talk about themselves, it honors who they are, it allows them to get to know their classmates, and it shows the value of talking as an essential piece to the drawing and writing process.

Getting Started

MATERIALS LIST:

For each student:

pencil, several sheets of paper, crayons

Additional materials: chart paper, markers

Suggested picture books about feelings:

My Many Colored Days by Dr. Seuss

What Are You So Grumpy About by Tom Lichtenheld

The Way I Feel by Janan Cain

When Sophie Gets Angry—Really, Really, Angry...
by Molly Bang

Today I Feel Silly: And Other Moods That Make My Day
by Jamie Lee Curtis

The Bad Mood by Amelie Jackowski

Lots of Feelings by Shelley Rotner

The Feelings Book by Todd Parr

Hurty Feelings by Helen Lester

Large-group instruction:

1. Introduce a book of your choice that shows characters with strong feelings. Discuss what parts of the face show the emotions. Compare several faces in the book and talk about the differences in emotions, as shown by different facial features. Look for books with large contrasts of emotions in the characters' faces.

2. Model drawing a face on a large surface. Ask students to suggest an emotion they saw in the book. Use the Pick and Draw game to direct which facial feature to draw next. Lightly draw or draw with pencil until students agree that the feature shows the right emotion.

3. Discuss. Which features were important for this emotion? Which were not important? Does the size of a feature make a difference in expressing emotion? For example, does a bigger mouth mean happier or madder?

DRAW

VARIATIONS:

1. Generate a discussion about strong feelings and what they look and sound like. Use chart paper to record student responses. Encourage specific rich language such as grumpy, irritated, frustrated, overjoyed, disheartened and delighted. Use PAD to draw faces and then match the face to the closest emotion word and place the drawings beside the appropriate word.

2. Use the PAD game to draw faces. Ask students to take turns acting out the emotion of the face s/he drew while the rest of the class tries to name the feeling.

3. Ask students to choose one of the emotion words and use the PAD game to draw the specific emotion on a face.

4. Study one of the children's books and discuss how the illustrator creates a specific emotion. Guide the students toward specific details, providing vocabulary when needed.

5. Extend the activity by asking students to tell and eventually write an emotional story. Discuss what a person would do, say or think if they were feeling a specific emotion such as excitement, nervousness, anxiety or ecstasy. Ask students to choose an emotion, close their eyes and think of a time s/he felt that emotion. Remind them to use rich feeling words. Now work toward drawing that story and, depending on the students' levels, work toward writing the story.

6. Learning centers. As students' skills develop, move the PAD game to a learning center and encourage students to draw faces, especially faces that express emotions, and talk, discuss and write about those emotions.

Discussion

THE SUCCESS of these activities depends partly on the teacher's modeling. Modeling involves demonstrating the specific actions and language patterns you want the students to use in their own work. Words alone are not enough. Often, children hear the right words for an action but struggle in the moment to actually follow through. Saying that they need to draw the eyes is not the same thing as showing them how to draw them. As they follow your demonstration, students begin to internalize the skills.

APRIL LARREMORE is a kindergarten and first-grade strategist. She has a master's degree in curriculum and instruction and is currently working on a doctorate in early-childhood studies. She has taught kindergarten for 14 years and has been an early-childhood strategist for the last two. She has done professional development on teaching little  ones to read and write for the last several years. She lives in Texas with her family. For more tips and ideas on working with young children, visit her blog, Chalk Talk, www.larremoreteachertips.blogspot.com.

Using Pick and Draw to Write Stories in an Hour

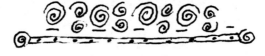

overview

WHEN STUDENTS create stories, they face difficulties with characters, plot and first drafts. This activity quickly creates individual characters, encourages students to become invested in their characters, rehearses a plot and gets a first draft down on paper. It can typically be completed in an hour. It uses Pick and Draw to combine several prewriting activities into an hour of intense but fun, productive work.

Background

FIRST STUDENTS will draw a character in five distinct steps using Pick and Draw. For each feature the student adds, they also add to a growing description of the character. At several points, they stop and tell a story about the character to a partner, doing an oral rehearsal of the story. After this rich prewriting that explores character and story, they are ready to write a first draft.

One reason this works is because the step-by-step progression creates a growing excitement and commitment to the character and story. Classic sales technique asks people to make a series of small decisions and commitments. When potential customers do this, it's easier for them to make the ultimate decision to buy. For example, encyclopedia salesmen used to ask people questions like this: What color set would you want? Where would you put the bookshelf to hold the series of books?

When we ask student writers to give the character a specific name, with a beginning, middle and last name, it's a similar commitment. It makes it easier for them to be committed to telling this story.

Because the activity is fast paced, it also circumvents the internal editor, that sneaky voice that tells you, "This is a dumb story." Instead, the fast pace and the excitement of the art keep students working. The excitement and growing success of their efforts pull them forward.

Getting Started

MATERIALS LIST:

For each student: pencil, several sheets of paper.
extra paper and sharpened pencils

Additional materials:
stop watch, kitchen timer or clock with a second hand.

FOR LARGE classes, divide the class into pairs to allow partners for storytelling. If there's an odd number, one group will need three people, and you'll have to allow an extra timed period for the third storyteller in the group.

Discussion

THE SUCCESS of this activity depends on a fast-paced, fun environment. Allow a fair amount of talking back and forth among students during the prewriting phase. However, that switches when students begin to write the first draft. Then, maintain silence for the entire writing time. The watchword here is, "Keep those pencils moving."

Students should write for the entire writing time and not stop until you call time. You must tell them this ahead of time. Often, a student will finish quickly, then use the remaining blank space at the end of a page to write a giant THE END. Warn them ahead that this is not acceptable! They must move the pencils across the page and not stop until you call time.

Decide ahead if you will direct the writing in a particular way. For example, if you are studying folk and fairy tales, you may want the characters to fit into that genre: trolls, kings, princesses, dwarfs, ogres, dragons, etc.

The oral storytelling is an effective prewriting tool. Consider asking the students to repeat their story, but this time tell it "a different way." This retelling sets up a mindset of revision: stories are fluid, and students can revise them to be better stories. Building revision into the oral storytelling step means students have a chance to rehearse the story several ways and decide on the best way to tell the story.

During the writing time, it's helpful to have extra paper and sharpened pencils available. Ask students to raise their hands quietly if they need one of these.

Instructions

1. **MOVE IT.** Divide students into pairs, with no more than eight groups.

2. **NAME IT.** Pass out the Face card, one to each group. Students should draw the face shape large enough to fill up at least half of the page; it should not be a small face. As soon as they have drawn the face shape, ask students to name their character. They must have a first name, middle name and last name. After each card, circulate among the students' desks and, as soon as most have named their character, move to the next step. Keep a fast pace.

3 HATE IT. Pass out the Nose cards, one to each group. (We have suggested an order to the feature cards, but vary this as needed.) Students add the feature to their drawing. Then ask them to number 1, 2, 3 and write three things the character hates or fears. For example, they may hate to eat broccoli, be scared of full moons and dislike wearing sandals.

Nose

OO I'M GREEN

4 LOVE IT. Pass out the Eye cards, one to each group. Students add the feature to their drawing. Now, students will number 1, 2, 3 and write three things the character loves. They will also do the first oral storytelling: the purpose of this storytelling is to tell something about the character's job or family.

Eyes

I'M PURPLE

PICK AND DRAW

CHARGE!

5. TELL IT:
Oral Storytelling

A. Each student should have a partner, and each group should decide which partner will talk first. Ask the students going first to hold up their hands and make sure each group knows who will start.

YADA
YADA
YADA

B. Instructions to students: You will be telling a story to your partner about your character. You will have one minute to tell the story and must talk for the entire minute. Partners, if the storyteller stops before I call time, ask questions to help them keep talking about the story. (Answer any questions that students have.)

C. Set the timer to one minute, start it and tell the students, "Go!" At 30 seconds, tell them, "Half the time is gone." At the end of one minute, call, "Stop!" Repeat, so the second partner can tell his/her story.

24

6 DARN IT. Pass out the Mouth cards, one to each group. Students add the feature to their drawing. Now the students will start thinking about the plot. Ask students to write down a problem that faces the character. For example, s/he may need to rescue a princess in distress, win a soccer game or convince Mom to let a friend spend the night.

7 TRY IT. Pass out the Hair cards, one to each group. Students add the feature to their drawing. Number 1, 2, 3: students will think of two ways a character might try to solve the problem but fail. After they do this, they can add a third attempt that will work. This is the basic plot, two things fail and a third thing works.

Oral Storytelling: This time, students will tell the story using the plot they just thought of.

Second Storytelling: Repeat the exercise, but this time, students must tell the story a different way. They can start at a different place, include new or different details, omit details or end at a different place.

Third Storytelling: If time allows and students aren't too restless, you can repeat a third time, asking students again to tell it a different way.

8. **WRITE IT.** Ask students to take out a clean sheet of paper for a first draft. They will write for an extended length of time: For younger students, 15 minutes; for older students, up to 30 minutes. They must "move the pencil across the page" for the entire time. They cannot end early and write THE END; they must keep moving the pencils until you call time. No talking allowed during this time. Set the timer and start it. Give regular updates. For example: 20 minutes left; half your writing time is gone so you should be about halfway finished writing; five minutes left, so you should be on your last paragraph.

TICK TOCK!

CELEBRATE IT! After an intense prewriting and drafting session like this, celebrate the progress the students have made on their stories! Plan to take time in the next session to revise.

DARCY PATTISON
(www.darcypattison.com)
is a children's book author and writing teacher. She has done professional development on the topic of teaching writing to kids for over 25 years. For more tips on prewriting activities see www. paperlightning.com.

A special thanks to Darcy for her help with this book. This book was her idea and inspiration. God has given you a special gift, Darcy! —RICH DAVIS

Using Pick and Draw to Answer What-are-you-like Questions

Overview

THIS ACTIVITY is good for beginning writers (younger grades) or for those students exploring character development in creative writing (older grades).

Background

GIVING FICTIONAL characters a personality is an essential ingredient in creative writing. Young students often remember to name their character or tell something about their character's family, but what really makes a character come alive involves defining the character's quirks and

interests. This activity is similar to those silly e-mail questionnaires that help you get to know your friends better. Beginning writers are not as intimidated by the writing process when they only have to write down a question and an answer. More experienced writers will gain experience in thinking through what makes their character "tick."

Getting Started

MATERIALS LIST:
Pick and Draw cards,
lined and unlined paper,
pencils
sample questionnaire (see pages 33-35)

Instructions

1. Give each student an unlined piece of paper and a pencil. Lead students through the Pick and Draw cartoon-drawing process, preferably having students draw as different a cartoon as possible from everyone else (which would involve letting students pick their own cards for each part of the drawing, but that is only recommended for students who have previous experience with the Pick and Draw process).

2. Talk to the students about how different each person in this world is and how each person would probably give different answers to the same questions. Give some examples of silly e-mail questionnaires that have been circulated in the past and how different people might answer them.

3. Explain that part of writing about a newly invented character involves inventing a personality as well. And it is important to do this because it will help the writer figure out how the character might respond to everyday situations as well as major life crises in the story where the character lives.

4. Have each student go back to looking at his or her Pick and Draw cartoon character. Have them think of something silly about him or her and then come up with a question that would elicit that response. For example, pretend that a newly invented character named Hubert craves Cherry Cokes with plenty of ice; the question that would have that answer is, "What is your favorite drink?"

5. Pool the questions into a classroom survey. The teacher can collect them in any way that fits the situation—write them all over the classroom chalkboard or have students submit them on 3x5 cards. If there are only a few students, then encourage each of them to think of two or three questions.

6. Have each student complete the classroom survey based on their own Pick and Draw character (who should also receive a name before, during or after this whole process).

7. If time allows, students can take turns introducing their characters to each other or to the whole class.

8. Bonus Activity: Graphing. If you are doing this activity with younger grades, use multiple-choice questions/answers for the classroom survey, and then help students explore graphing. This is very fun if floor space with large tiles is available—each student can lay his/her Pick and Draw character paper down in a line (one paper per tile) to make a bar graph on the floor. For example:

Question: What kind of pet does your character have or want?

- a) a dog
- b) a cat
- c) a parrot or parakeet
- d) aquarium fish
- e) something else

The bar graph would have five lines (one for each of the answers) for students to stand in with their Pick and Draw character, and once they found the right line to stand in, each student would put their paper down on a floor tile and back up to view the graph. After the teacher discusses it briefly, each student would pick up his/her Pick and Draw character and get ready for the next question.

Using multiple choice is not the BEST process for this activity because it limits creativity. For a classroom of very creative children (every teacher's dream, right?), then the graph would have a much longer line for the answer "e) something else" because that is where all the characters who wanted zebras or giraffes or monkeys or boa constrictors would have to stand. Not a bad thing, really, but depending on the questions, it can really skew the graphing data.

32

GET-TO-KNOW-YOUR-FRIENDS
Survey

* Name: _____

1. What time did you get up this morning?
2. Diamonds or pearls?
3. What was the last movie you saw at a theater?
4. What is your favorite T.V. show?
5. What did you have for breakfast?
6. What is your middle name?
7. Favorite cuisine or food?
8. What food do you dislike?
9. What is your favorite color?
10. What is your favorite CD at the moment?
11. What kind of car do you drive?
12. Favorite lunch?
13. What characteristics in people do you dislike?
14. Your favorite past-time is:
15. If you could go anywhere in the world on vacation, where would you go?
16. Who is your favorite singer?
17. Favorite brand of clothing?
18. To where would you retire?
19. What was your most memorable birthday?
20. Favorite sport to watch?
21. Goal you have for yourself?
22. When is your birthday?

23. How many weddings have you been in, including your own?

24. Are you a morning person or a night person?

25. What is your shoe size?

26. Pets:

27. Any new and exciting news you'd like to share with us?

28. What did you want to be when you were little?

29. How do you feel today?

30. What is your favorite candy?

31. What is your favorite plant or flower?

32. What day on the calendar are you looking forward to?

33. Where is the farthest you have ever been from home?

34. A small thing you really enjoy?

35. What is your favorite book?

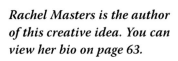

Rachel Masters is the author of this creative idea. You can view her bio on page 63.

36. What are you most proud of?
37. What is your favorite album?
37. What makes you cringe?
38. If you could do anything, what would you do?
39. Where have you been that you will visit again?
40. Where have you been that you will never visit again?
41. Which came first, the chicken or the egg?
42. How many people have you made smile today?
43. When you look at the world, what do you see?
44. Cats or Dogs?
45. Good or bad?
46. Something people probably don't know about you?

Why should people have all the fun?!
c'mon–
Let's go play Pick and Draw ourselves!

Illustrating Idioms Using Pick and Draw

Overview

THE ENGLISH language includes several phrases that cannot be translated literally. These idioms can present special difficulties for English-as-a-Second-Language students and early elementary students and deserve special attention when studying the English language.

Background

WHEN STUDENTS try to interpret an idiom literally, they can create a humorous mental picture. Using cartoon characters to represent these silly ideas is a fun way to highlight or review a study of idioms. Collecting miniature illustrations in a small photo album can turn this into an ongoing project over several weeks or months.

Getting Started

MATERIALS LIST:

Pick and Draw cards,

unlined paper or card stock,

pencils AND colored pencils or markers,

a list of idioms from the English language
(pages 40-41),

small photo album for each student (optional)

Instructions

1. Give each student an unlined piece of paper and a pencil. Lead students through the Pick and Draw cartoon-drawing process, preferably having students draw as different a cartoon as possible from everyone else (which would involve letting students pick their own cards for each part of the drawing, but that is only recommended for students who have previous experience with the Pick and Draw process). Give them time to name their character and color them as desired.

2. Remind students that idioms are phrases that should not be translated literally, but if they were, they would have entirely different meanings. Use one of the idioms on pages 40-41 to illustrate on the board using a sample cartoon character.

38

3. Give students time to illustrate an idiom of their own using an idiom from the provided list or thinking of their own, using their own cartoon character. Remind them to draw lightly at first, especially since they are adding in background details to give a literal meaning to their idiom. At the bottom of the page, they should clearly write their chosen idiom along with a proper definition, either in their own words or copied from a children's dictionary.

4. To use this as a one-time activity, have each student illustrate a different idiom, then collect the cartoon drawings and display them as a group. To use this as an ongoing project for each student, have them use card stock cut into four pieces (trimmed to be 4" wide by 5½" long) for each illustration, completing one or two different idioms during each session. Students can insert each small card-stock page into a small photo album until the album is filled.

Rachel Masters is the author of this creative idea. You can view her bio on page 63.

FAMILIAR IDIOMS OF THE ENGLISH LANGUAGE

- Don't cry over spilled milk.
- Don't judge a book by its cover.
- Eaten out of house and home.

- Get a taste of your own medicine.
- Get up on the wrong side of the bed.
- You can't teach an old dog new tricks.

- Two heads are better than one.
- Turn over a new leaf.
- Beggars can't be choosers.

- Look before you leap.
- One rotten apple spoils the whole barrel.
- The show must go on.

- His bark is worse than his bite.
- Beat around the bush.
- Giving me the cold shoulder.

- That's the last straw.
- The straw that broke the camel's back.
- It's on its last legs.
- Rule the roost.

- Make hay while the sun shines.
- Birds of a feather flock together.
- Bull in a china shop.

◢ Money burning a hole in your pocket.
◢ Once in a blue moon.
◢ Don't put all your eggs in one basket.

◢ Kill two birds with one stone.
◢ Bite the hand that feeds you.
◢ 'Til the cows come home.

◢ Make a mountain out of a molehill.
◢ Sit on the fence.
◢ Take the bull by the horns.

◢ Every cloud has a silver lining.
◢ Out of the frying pan and into the fire.
◢ Great oaks from little acorns grow.

◢ A watched pot never boils.
◢ Catch forty winks.
◢ Chip on your shoulder.

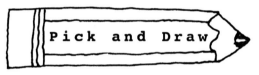

Pick and Draw

◢ Steal his thunder.
◢ Hit the nail on the head.
◢ Let the cat out of the bag.

◢ Don't look a gift horse in the mouth.
◢ Cost an arm and a leg.
◢ Couch potato.

◢ Can of worms.
◢ Beat a dead horse.
◢ Easy as pie.

◢ Between a rock and a hard place.
◢ Can't see the forest for the trees.

Rachel Masters is the author of this creative idea. You can view her bio on page 63.

41

Using Pick and Draw to Teach Nonfiction Writing

Overview

STUDENTS TODAY must learn to deal with facts and information as they write nonfiction. To illustrate the importance of the writer in the process, Pick and Draw provides a graphic way to show them how changing one fact changes the entire "picture" of nonfiction writing.

Background

AS A NONFICTION writer, I deal with facts and information to weave a coherent, interesting story. But I am also aware of how important the individual writer is to the process.

Discussion

THIS IS A good introduction to writing informative, descriptive or argument essays as well as research reports. The emphasis here is on how the writer affects the way information is conveyed when written. It can also be used to emphasize the importance of a writer's voice in any type of writing because it makes visible individual differences.

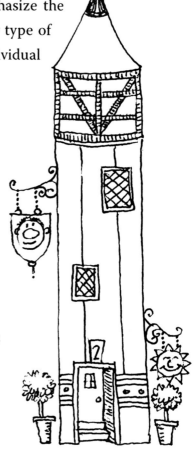

Getting Started

MATERIALS LIST:
Pick and Draw game,
white copier paper,
pencils with erasers

Instructions

USING THE Pick and Draw cards, follow the directions to have students draw faces. The whole class will draw from the same face cards.

As the students draw each feature on their own paper, you should also draw on a white board. When all the elements are drawn, have the students look at their neighbor's picture and ask these questions:

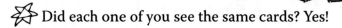 Did each one of you see the same cards? Yes!

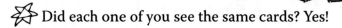 Did each one of you draw the same shapes? Yes!

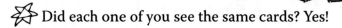 Does your picture look the same as your neighbor's? No!

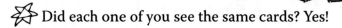 Do they look similar? Some yes, some no!

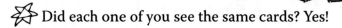 Do they look different? Some yes, some no!

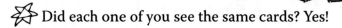 What is different about each one?

If everyone had the same cards and everyone drew the same shapes, why don't each of your pictures look exactly the same?

What is the ONLY thing that is different? **YOU!**

44

Discussion

DISCUSS THE fact that each student had the same information but used that information in a different way. This is why different people can write books on the same topic, and they will all be different.

Once the students understand this concept, move to the next phase. When you write nonfiction, you do research to find out facts about your topic. Imagine that each feature of the Pick and Draw game represents one fact. The face shape is one fact, the nose another fact, the mouth another fact, and the hair another. Depending on the age of the students, give examples about how much variety you could have using only four facts.

Make sure the students understand that each feature in the picture represents one fact. Then tell them that you're going to take away one of the facts and replace it with another fact. Ask one student to draw a different card for a mouth. On the white board, erase the first mouth and replace it with a different mouth. Ask students to do the same on their pictures, then ask these questions:

⭐ Did the picture change when we added a different mouth? Yes!

⭐ Were both pictures accurate, even though they looked different? Yes!

⭐ Nonfiction writing revolves around doing research to find out facts, then choosing which of those facts to use.

Depending on which research facts you choose to use, your nonfiction "picture" will look different.

⚝ Using the Pick and Draw game is a good way to illustrate to students how to use facts to write nonfiction.

CARLA KILLOUGH MCCLAFFERTY is an award-winning author of nonfiction books. She is available to speak at schools, teacher conferences, professional-development workshops and civic organizations. She tailors her presentations to fit the needs of the audience. As the author of informational texts, she is frequently invited to present information on how to find primary source documents and then use that information to write accurate and interesting text. She also speaks about the lives of the people she has written about. Her books include *Tech Titans, The Many Faces of George Washington: Remaking a Presidential Icon, In Defiance of Hitler: The Secret Mission of Varian Fry, Something Out of Nothing: Marie Curie and Radium, The Head Bone's Connected to the Neck Bone: The Weird, Wacky and Wonderful X-ray*, and *Forgiving God*. For more information visit her website at www.carlamcclafferty.com.

Pick and Draw cowboy caricature

overview

A WORKSHEET guide to help students prepare for a creative writing project, specifically based on a fictitious cowboy, but adaptable to other characters as well. Ideal for grades three and up.

Background

WHEN WE were studying American history in our homeschool, we read books about cowboys and sang cowboy ballads, but I wanted to give my oldest two children (in fifth and sixth grades) a chance to expand their imaginations by creating their own cowboy character for a story. They would use the Pick and Draw cards to create their cowboy characters.

The worksheet on page 55 is my attempt at helping them do some brainstorming instead of staring at a blank page. My son and my daughter were both excited to do this project, but my son, Nathan, took it to the extreme. His cowboy, named Anvil, seemed to take on a life of his own, and Nathan ended up writing and illustrating several more chapters in the life of Anvil over the rest of the school year. It was wonderful to have a simple project spark such creativity.

Getting Started

MATERIALS LIST:

nonfiction books about the life of a cowboy,

cowboy props (optional),

movie clips of cowboys (optional)
*For example, scenes from Old Western movies
(NOT including violence),*

Pick and Draw cards

one copy of the following worksheet for each student,

pencils AND colored pencils or crayons,

lined and unlined paper

Instructions

1. Spend some time teaching students about the life of a cowboy, using the nonfiction books and any props or movie clips available. Explain vocabulary words that are specific to the life of a cowboy and write them in a visible location so that students can use these words in their story. For instance:

CHAPS LIL' DOGGIES STAMPEDE CORRAL CHUCKWAGON RODEO

Don't be tempted to skimp on this part. Imaginations flow better when there is plenty of ACCURATE information to draw from. However, make these learning sessions captivating to the students. Sing (or play) cowboy songs, relate short stories of real-life cowboys, get them hooked on the Old West with edge-of-your-seat true happenings from the cowtowns of the late 1800s. Show pictures of not-so-famous cowboys facing dusty trails with big herds of Longhorn cattle. This portion of the teaching should take several hours, spread out over several days, in order to have the creative juices really flowing.

Don't leave HOME without it

50

2. Get out the unlined paper and pencils and explain that it is their turn to create their own cowboy. Use the Pick and Draw cards to lead students through the process of creating a face to go with their cowboy or cowgirl. Emphasize the need to draw lightly with their pencils since they will be adding to the finished product.

3. It is time to complete the cowboy caricature by adding a tiny body. It may be helpful to show examples of caricatures of famous people so that students understand that a large head and a small body are part of "the look." If cowboy props are available (such as hats or boots or spurs), be sure to show them to the students at this point. Adding a cowboy hat to a face that is already drawn can be a challenge for beginning art students—consider drawing an example on the board so that students can see how to erase some parts in order to add others. Give the students time to color their drawings. Depending on the age of your students, they could do some parts of this assignment as homework. It will take at least one class session.

4. Personality development: Ask each student to really examine the cowboy caricature s/he has drawn. Using a blank piece of paper and a pencil, ask them to list several aspects of their cowboy's personality. Is the cowboy brave or cowardly? What does he like to eat for supper? Is he generally cheerful or annoyed? Questions like these bring out distinctions that will make their characters come to life. It is important to know what the cowboy's distinct quirks are in order to imagine how he will react to the problems he needs to solve.

5. Hand out the following worksheet to each student. This is the brainstorming part of the project to prepare them for writing their creative stories. Depending on the students' skill levels, it may be helpful to do part or all of this worksheet together as a class. But creativity would flow best if students did NOT have to share all of their ideas with each other. This is supposed to be a UNIQUE work of art, which means that each student should dig deep within himself to find ideas. Students who are excited about this project will likely not want to STOP, while reluctant students may not know where to START. (Good luck!) It is not necessary to write complete sentences on this worksheet. Neither should it be graded, but do look at it before the students start on their writing project to see if they've made a good skeleton to build on before going any farther.

6. Turn them loose with their writing project without delay. It is best to let students get at it right away while enthusiasm is high. The first draft of any creative story is likely to be messy and full of mistakes, but encourage them to get their ideas on paper before they forget anything. Allow plenty of time for this writing assignment, either during class sessions or at home.

7. As students finish the first draft, they should set it aside for a few days, if possible, before going on to polish the first draft into a finished product. Often when students come back to a story after letting it sit, they are able to see mistakes better—areas where their story just doesn't flow right or where they skipped a word. If the students REALLY like the drawing part, they can add a few more pictures for interest. Consider having students type

their story or rewrite it neatly, as appropriate for their skill or age levels.

8. If at all possible, find a way to share these stories with SOMEONE. Read them aloud to the class, a few at a time, if it's appropriate. Or put them into a three-ring binder for classmates to read. Or publish one or two of them in a school newspaper. Each teacher knows their students and what type of sharing would let them know that their stories are interesting and worthwhile reading.

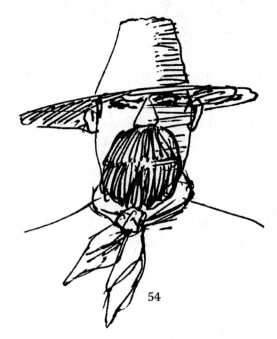

WRITING ASSIGNMENT: COWBOY CARICATURE

THIS WEEK we're studying cowboys and the wide, wild west. Your assignment is to create a cowboy caricature and write a story to go with him or her. Use the Pick and Draw cards to draw a large cartoon face. Then add a small body, dressed like a cowboy. Give him a name and a personality, and then fill in these blanks to start coming up with a story. When you have finished your final draft, we'll display them for others to read.

#1: What are some things that a cowboy wears?
   What types of items does he use to do his job?

_____

_____

_____

_____

#2: What animals do you usually think of with cowboys?
   What would be an unusual pet for a cowboy?

_____

_____

_____

_____

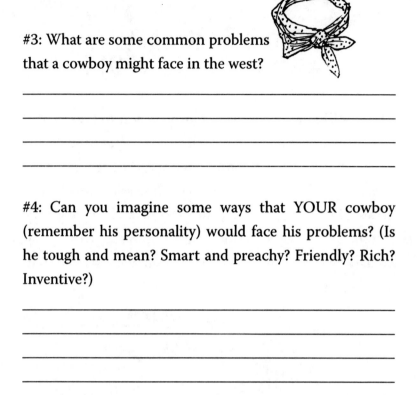

#3: What are some common problems that a cowboy might face in the west?

_____

_____

_____

_____

#4: Can you imagine some ways that YOUR cowboy (remember his personality) would face his problems? (Is he tough and mean? Smart and preachy? Friendly? Rich? Inventive?)

_____

_____

_____

_____

The basic recipe for a good story is to create a character with his own personality, give him a friend or two, get him into a problem, then explain how he gets OUT of his problem, and give the story a nice, happy ending. Or for a tragedy, make the ending sad. Do a good job on your cartoon picture, and type your story.

Rachel Masters is the author of this creative idea. You can view her bio on page 63.

Pick and Draw Postcards from Armchair Travelers

overview

STUDENTS WHO cannot afford world travel can still pretend to visit other places through studying geography. Super imposing a cartoon avatar on pictures of familiar landmarks can give students a "Postcards from Buster" feel as they learn about different places.

DAVIS

58

Background

WHEN WE studied the countries of the eastern hemisphere in homeschool this past year, I discovered anew all the places in the world that tourists dream of visiting, such as the Great Wall of China or the Taj Mahal. The chances that my children or I will ever actually visit these places are miniscule, which means we may never have a picture of ourselves standing near these famous landmarks. But with all the images available through the Internet or good travel books, it is relatively easy to "cut and paste" a cartoon character onto the corner of any photo. Adding in a small (or large) amount of research means that students can write a postcard to anyone, pretending that they have visited any famous landmark in the world.

Discussion

THIS COULD easily incorporate technology if that is an educational goal for the year. Students could take an active role in finding the appropriate photographs of famous landmarks from the Internet and then learn to use a photo-editing program to digitally "cut and paste" as many times as they like. If money is no object, they could even create a digital memory book to document their armchair traveling adventures. The Internet may provide free options.

Getting Started

MATERIALS LIST:

Pick and Draw cards,

unlined paper,

pencils AND colored pencils or markers,

scissors and glue,

photos of famous landmarks (or landscapes)
from the geographical area being studied,

nonfiction books that give accurate information
about the countries or landmarks being studied,

access to a photocopier (optional)

Younger students may enjoy reading *Flat Stanley* or watching an episode of "Postcards from Buster" to get a feel for imaginary traveling. This will add significant time before actually initiating the project described below.

Instructions

1. Lead students through the Pick and Draw process to create a cartoon character. Each student can try for a normal-looking cartoon that resembles himself OR each student can create an outrageous cartoon character that will travel the world in STYLE! Remind them to draw lightly with pencil until they are satisfied with their character. Students should pick a name if they are representing someone other than themselves.

BULLY!
Just
BULLY!

2. If the class includes advanced artists, encourage them to draw several poses of their character, dressed as a tourist. They could draw their character with outstretched arms, looking pensive or pointing toward something in the distance. These would all be of the SAME cartoon character, just different body poses, as if they themselves were posing for a picture in front of a famous landmark. Some poses should face slightly left and some should face slightly toward the right.

3. Depending on how many landmark photos are available for each student, consider making photocopies of their cartoon character. These might need to be reduced in size also. This will allow them to color, cut and paste indefinitely without having to re-draw their tourist cartoon characters repeatedly.

4. Display the available photos of landmarks and ask each student to choose one to research. If this is an extended project, they can choose several landmarks to research.

5. Students can use scissors and glue to put their cartoon character in the corner, to the side or smack-dab in the middle of each famous landmark photograph that they have chosen. To give it a real postcard feel, paste the photograph on one side of card stock and have students write on the other side of the card stock, including addresses and an imaginary postage stamp and cancellation mark.

6. If this is a technology project, instruct students in cutting and pasting using a digital photo-editing program so that they can create their own photos to use in a report or PowerPoint slide show.

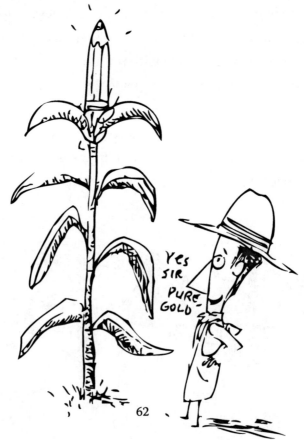

RACHEL MASTERS was raised on a farm in Iowa, and after living more than a decade in northwest Arkansas, she and her family moved back to the same community in Iowa. She and her husband, Darren, have been married 18 years and have six growing children at home. She homeschools the four oldest, helps manage Darren's  handyman construction business, sells the cookbook that she authored several years ago (see www.schallertel.net/~rmasters), stays actively involved in the local Evangelical Free Church, and TRIES to remember to enjoy all the duties that are involved in being a homemaker. They are raising their kids on an old farmplace that used to belong to her great-grandfather, and she loves living in the country.

When Rachel was in college at John Brown University, she majored in elementary education, with an emphasis in special education, and minored in math and social studies. Rachel taught only one year in a public school but has continued to be involved with other avenues of educating youngsters. It is one of her passions in life.

You may contact her at:
Rachel Masters
3650 Buchanan Ave.
Kiron, Iowa 51448
rmasters@schallertel.net

Making Educational Posters with Pick and Draw

Overview

THIS IS helpful when students need to learn and communicate dos and don'ts for a particular subject, such as health issues or classroom procedures.

Background

LEARNING THE rules of any subject can be rather dry and repetitive. This project adds some interest (and hopefully longer retention) for the students while giving the teacher some easy-to-display posters for the classroom or hallway.

Discussion

YOU CAN incorporate this activity into almost any learning situation in a variety of ways. The following page will feature examples from a health unit for fifth graders, using cooperative-learning groups, but you can also conduct this activity with the entire class (each student uses the same basic cartoon character but illustrates a different rule on each poster, or each student creates his or her own cartoon character and illustrates several rules on mini posters).

Getting Started

MATERIALS LIST:
Pick and Draw cards,
a list of rules
(teacher-made or brainstormed with students),
unlined paper, pencils,
poster board,
markers

Instructions

1. Give each cooperative-learning group a chance to invent a new character using the Pick and Draw cards. They need to take some time and work together to give their character a name and a unique look. Students can do this initial drawing with pencil and unlined paper, drawing lightly so they can erase and re-draw until they are satisfied with their character.

2. Ideally, all students will be familiar with the dos and don'ts of the subject at hand from previous classroom discussions. The rules they're illustrating shouldn't need long explanations but a simple review. Give each group a list of rules (one or two per student) to illustrate on their posters.

3. Each student in the cooperative-learning group can start to sketch out their idea for an illustration, including a conversation bubble that names the rule. Students should strive to make their cartoon faces consistent within the group, even if the cartoon bodies are performing different activities.

4. When students are satisfied with their initial sketches, hand out the poster board and markers so students can make their final project. If you want smaller displays, consider using card stock, and cut around the illustrations, then mount each group's collection of rules on the same poster board.

Rachel Masters is the author of this creative idea. You can view her bio on page 63.

Pick and Draw Art Activity...a fun way to Practice the Basics

overview

THIS IS A GROUP ACTIVITY that provides everyone with something different to do simultaneously. Kids interact as a group but still have the opportunity to be individual in their creative expression.

At the end of this activity, every student will have a cartoon face that they have created as well as many practice attempts with the different kinds of lines that create the parts that make the face.

Background

YOUNG STUDENTS need practice of the basics to continue growing and learning in order to build confidence. Students with a low sense of confidence won't explore creatively. They need a fun way to practice the drawing basics with good results in a short time. Here's an activity to help.

I believe the key is to combine playing a game, using cartoons and providing opportunities for individual creative exploration. This activity delivers all three.

It is also meant to move at a fast pace and provide a short, fun warm-up time at the beginning of class. Students need to stay challenged so they don't bog down in repetition.

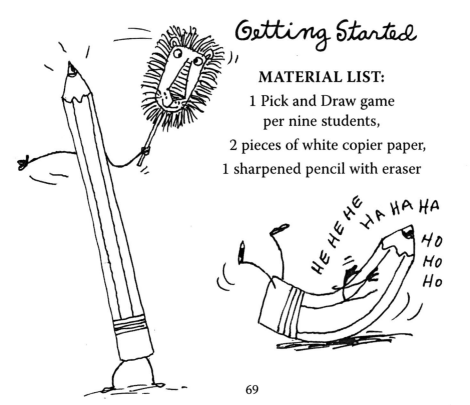

Getting Started

MATERIAL LIST:
1 Pick and Draw game
per nine students,
2 pieces of white copier paper,
1 sharpened pencil with eraser

Instructions

DEPENDING ON the number of students in your class/group, divide into groups of three sitting around a table. If no tables are available, you might clump desks (chairs) to face each other. If possible, have the seating arranged beforehand with paper and pencil at each place so that you can jump into the activity quickly. Keep it simple, and keep it moving.

INTRODUCTION TO ACTIVITY

THIS INFORMATION is taken from the book *Drawing with Children* by Mona Brookes, which was published in 1986 by J.P. Tarcher Publishing Co. The 10th anniversary edition, which was published in 1996 by Putnam Publishing Co, can be purchased at any book store or through amazon.com. Both *Drawing with Children* and *Drawing for Older Children and Teens* by Mona Brookes will give you more information on how to use the five Elements of Shape. I am going to introduce you to the five Elements of Shape that you can use to draw anything.

First explain that everything in the world can be drawn using five things we already know how to make. Then on a dry-erase or chalk board, write in large letters...

voic

Then define the five for them:

V is an angle line

O is a circle

. is a dot

I is a straight line

C is a curve line

When you use these lines in drawing, you can speak; you have a "voice."

Depending on how much interaction you desire, you can take this into an interactive time by asking what other letters in the alphabet use these five things (any letter or number will work). Take a letter and draw it up on the board, using an A for example, then show how it is made by using an angle line (upside-down V) and a straight line going across in the middle of the letter. You can refer to this as an "angle-

PICK and DraW

straight" to make the letter. Let them choose a couple of other letters and draw them out slowly, letting them define what Elements of Shape they need to make them. Then let them try some other letters on their own and see if they can define the elements they need to make them. This will set them up for the Pick and Draw activity. This activity is teaching them to recognize the five elements and to practice them, and finally to make a cartoon face with them. When you feel like they understand this concept, then move into the Pick and

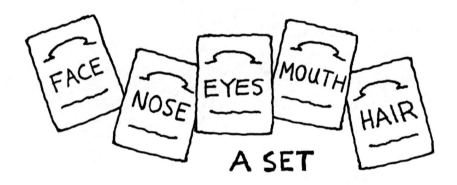

A SET

MOVING TO PICK AND DRAW

GIVE EACH PERSON in the group a set of cards. A set consists of one of each of the five color cards (face, nose, eyes, mouth and hair). Instruct the students not to look at the cards yet. Have the cards in a stack kept in this order: red on top, green, purple, blue and last orange. Thus, each student has their own stack of five cards; two pieces of white copier paper and a pencil with an eraser if possible.

READY, Go!

WHEN YOU SAY "begin," each student will flip over their top card and draw it, thinking about what kind of elements it uses from the five you just gave them. Have them draw that shape on the paper as many times as they can (not messy) for a short length of time, maybe 30-45 seconds. Tell them to stop when the time is up and ask them to turn over the second card. Repeat what you did with the first card, reminding them to think about which of the five elements they use to make that shape. Keep it moving through all five of the cards. They can use the front and back of the paper to practice the shapes on the cards.

FACE IT!

ON THE SECOND piece of paper, have them combine the shapes to make a cartoon face as a timed activity. If you feel you need to really challenge them, then have them flip their paper over and draw another cartoon face using the same five cards, but this time it has to look different because they changed the size or position of those shapes. Have them go back and name their characters and add any extras they want to make it funnier (freckles, glasses, beard, etc). Let them show and tell their works of art.

They are ready to move into some other art activity now; they are all warmed up!

Discussion

IT WOULD BE VALUABLE for the students to hear and see what kind of elements (from V O i C) they used to make the parts for the face. When they really get the concept of breaking down everything we see into these elements, it will empower them. Discussion about this and letting them visually show their practice will give them confidence, and I would imagine that when they leave your class, their eyes will be more attentive to seeing what kinds of elements make up everything around them.

Reinforce the need for "practice" and "warm up" in order to get better at anything. Maybe they will want to tell you what other things they do where warm up or practice would help. In this way, you are introducing or reinforcing a life skill. Art allows you a visual payoff at the end of the activity, which can bring the payoff of new confidence.

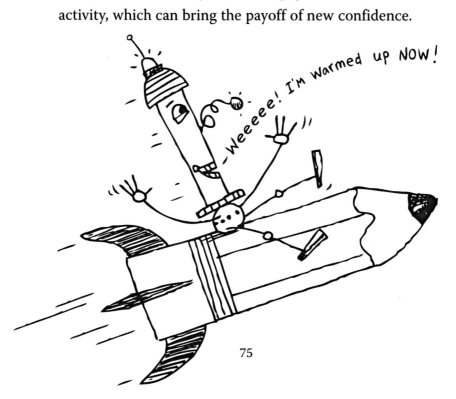

Weeeeee! I'M warmed up NOW!

Pick and Draw with Clay: Opening the Door to 3D Thinking

USS PICK AND DRAW

overview

USUALLY PICK AND DRAW emphasizes creativity with pencil/pen and paper. This activity, however, gives kids a piece of clay to play with. The result will be a clay model of a Pick and Draw face—with the possibility of adding a body and other props.

Background

PEOPLE ARE ENRICHED when they begin to think in three dimensions. This is the ability to imagine objects and to turn them around in your imagination to view them from different angles. This activity practices 3D thinking and results in an idea becoming an object to hold.

BENEFITS I HAVE SEEN FROM THIS PROJECT:

1. Helps students design something that is specific and original

2. Helps students see objects three dimensionally in their imagination

3. Fosters self-exploration

4. Reinforces "process" as a means of doing something well

5. Provides fun opportunities for problem solving

6. Helps students value tools to complete a task with higher skill

7. Helps students feel a part of a group with a single focus but also lets each person have a unique contribution

A "lifetime learner" is someone who continually tries to see things from different angles, different perspectives. They are always looking around the next corner. This activity reinforces and illustrates an open attitude toward learning. That openness can also spill over to relationships and help prevent discrimination and prejudice (narrow, 2D thinking). In this way, art can be a powerful learning tool for life skills.

Getting Started

MATERIALS LIST:

Pick and Draw game (for whole class)

Per student:

1 sheet of standard white copier paper,

1 pencil with eraser,

1 saucer-size styrofoam plate
(to put their finished sculpture on for drying, display and identification),

1 palm-size hunk of an air-dry clay, such as Crayola Air-dry, a little smaller than a tennis ball

Provide a selection of simple objects that students can use as tools: paper clip, small tongue depressor, ball-point pen cap, or anything else that comes to mind that might teach resourcefulness. Encourage students to see objects around them that have textures or shapes that could shape their clay. Art supply stores also have cheap clay tools you can buy in bulk.

Instructions

This activity is broken into two or three parts, which could be spread over a week (with 45 minute to one hour of class time each day). If your students only come once a week, then plan on two to four class periods, depending on your students' pace or how you extend the project.

1. Drawing the Pick and Draw cartoon characters and choosing one favorite

Take a clean piece of white copier paper, fold it "hamburger style," folding the long vertical down to make a half sheet. Next, fold in half the opposite way to create a miniature book (this is called "French fold" in the greeting card world).

Using the Pick and Draw game's basic instructions (white cards in the deck), lead the whole class in making four different cartoon faces, one on each of the four parts of the French fold: outside cover, inside left, inside right and outside back. Ask students to name each character. From the four faces, students should choose their favorite.

Optional: If time allows, ask students to redraw their favorite face on another full-size piece of paper but also add a body under the face. They can detail the body as they choose with clothes and shoes, etc. This additional drawing will help them make the change from paper to clay.

Pick Pick Pick and DRAW!

2. Making the clay sculpture

The goal is for students to think in 3D, not just draw into the clay. Begin with a discussion of the three dimensions of height, width and depth. Ask students to walk around another person and point out what parts stick out and what parts go in. They should learn to see three dimensions and then work to recreate this in their sculpture.

After introducing the concept of 3D, demonstrate how to work with clay and a couple of tools. One demonstration might be the difference between a free-standing sculpture (3D) and a relief sculpture (2D, like a picture, where you only see one side of the face) so students can choose a beginning point.

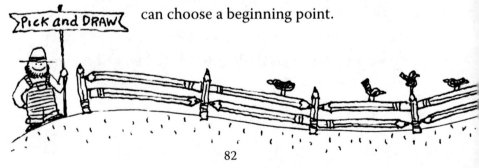

Pick and DRAW

Start with a clay ball just smaller than a tennis ball and cut it in three equal parts. Use one-third for shaping the head, one-third for the body and one-third for adding on extras like hair, eyes, nose, ears, hats, etc.

Demonstrate how to attach a piece of clay onto the main structure so that the joint is fairly strong. This would mean simply taking a tool that you can use to press down the edges where the two meet until you do not see any cracks.

One important factor is knowing when it is better to add a piece of clay and when it is better to shape it out of the existing ball of clay. A nose or an open mouth may be better shaped from the main ball of clay. Ears and hair may be better added onto the head. Warn students that small, thin shapes that are added on are easy to break on a finished sculpture.

83

Finally, demonstrate tools for detail work. Besides developing eye-hand coordination, tools can encourage students to be resourceful as they re-purpose an object as a tool to shape their clay. Perhaps the cap off of a ball-point pen will be a useful tool. Use what is at hand in your environment to shape the clay.

Ask students to create a 3D version of their chosen face. As individual problems arise, discuss the decision process freely so the entire class will benefit.

Tip: When students work on their clay, be sure that they can lift it off that surface and place it on their styrofoam saucer so that when they leave, the sculptures can be safely stored. Be sure each saucer is labeled with the student's name.

Optional: Some art is created to be observed, and some art has a certain function. As an option, students might consider the function of their sculptures. Maybe the sculpture is also a pen/pencil holder or a toothbrush holder or Christmas ornament. Brainstorm out loud one or two ways functionality might work into the sculpture's design, but verbally encourage original ideas about functional objects.

3. Drying time depends on the thickness of the sculptures. Allow three days if you are going to paint the sculptures afterwards or if you are letting students take them home. You might time their completion to be on Parent/Teacher night so that parents can help their child carry their sculpture home.

Extension activity:

After the sculptures have dried, paint the sculptures with acrylic paints. This takes the project to another level with the addition of wet media and paint brushes, another universally favorite activity for kids. Painting adds originality and the student's emotional investment in the project—it will be something they are proud of and want to show others.

Practical Note:

After the sculptures dry, when students begin to handle them, pieces will inevitably snap or fall off. Have super glue handy for repairs, which will often create stronger bonds than before. Head this off by cautioning students against attaching small, thin pieces to their sculpture. But be prepared anyway!

Discussion

This activity is rich in design principles, and a discussion will encourage students to think beyond this one project to general art principles. Here are some suggested topics for discussion or for writing a reflection essay.

1. What is the difference between 2D and 3D art?

2. Talk about using your imagination to see and turn objects around in different angles in order to study them.

3. What is special about working with clay and your hands?

4. What did you use to create textures in the clay? Which was faster to make, the drawing or the sculpture? Why?

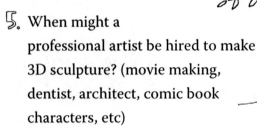

5. When might a professional artist be hired to make 3D sculpture? (movie making, dentist, architect, comic book characters, etc)

6. Can you think of a famous sculpture artist? (Michelangelo) Did he use clay?

7. Talk about how many choices you made during the process of sculpting. How did you decide what to do next?

8. Are you surprised how well you did with clay? How did you like working with clay and tools?

9. What do you like best about your sculpture?

10. What was the hardest part for you with this sculpture?

11. Are you going to give your sculpture to someone or keep it?

12. What would you do to make your sculpture better if you did it over?

13. If you did another clay sculpture, do you have any ideas what you could make?

RICH DAVIS is a creative specialist who also happens to illustrate children's books, combine traditional and digital art, make products for mass media and invent simple creative games. He serves as a teaching artist for the Arkansas Arts Council. Rich draws with thousands of children each year in different settings, experimenting with ways to unlock fears, empower experimentation and release kids into new ways to create with joy and excitement. He feels that confidence is a key factor in growing creatively, and he enjoys facilitating activities that give each person an enjoyable and successful experience. Using the Pick and Draw game ranks as one of the highest in learning and enjoyment among the resources that he has developed.

download

Downloadable "Activity cards" for Grief counseling with Teens or Art Education

overview

GRIEVING TEENS often have a difficult time putting their feelings into words. Teens may struggle to talk about their loved one's death—the hows, whys, etc. They may be feeling very different from others in their family, even though they are also grieving. By using the "activity cards," we are able to let teens in a group setting see that even though we all see the same thing, we all do something different with it. Just like their unique grief experience! As a family, we are all grieving, but we express our grief differently.

Getting Started

MATERIALS LIST:

Printed Activity Cards from

www.richdavis.freewebspace.com/box_widget.html,

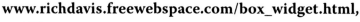

writing paper/construction paper,

markers or pen

Instructions

IN A GROUP setting: The group facilitator tells the group to draw what they see on the card onto their paper. Have them only focus on their paper. Do about 15 cards.

Discussion

HAVE THEM SHARE their pictures with the group.

Ask them the following:

1. What do you notice about the pictures?
2. What are the similarities?
3. What are the differences?
4. How are the styles different?
5. Did some people take the image and draw it exactly like they saw it? Or were they creative with the image?

Discuss:

1. Everyone saw the same image.
2. Point out that what each person did with the image is different—give a few examples.

Discuss the connection of this activity to grief. We are all grieving the death of someone we love; however, our grief looks different, just like these pictures. Some people may feel very angry, some may have no anger. Some people may feel very tired, while others have lots of extra energy. Discuss how we express grief is expressed differently, even among family members. Ask them if their family were here, would their pictures be different? Share with them that grief is a journey and that it is not a journey to travel alone.

Activity Cards for Art Ed

BESIDES USING THE ACTIVITY cards for grief counseling teens, they can also be used as an art activity in the classroom. It can serve as a fast-paced eye-hand coordination activity. As students look at the card you hold up each time, have them draw that card doodle on their paper just as they see it. Move through the cards at a good pace. Give them verbal permission to vary the sizes of their doodles to make their picture more interesting: or make the elements touch or stay apart. They can combine these to make something recognizable or keep the overall image abstract and random. Have them add two doodles of their own at the end as a bonus. This activity is great for honing their memory of things they see and learning to put them down quickly with growing accuracy. It also puts them in a repeating situation that stimulates design decisions with very little time...reactionary.

When they are done, have everyone lay their drawings out together and talk about the differences of expressions. Reinforce that each person's creativity has it's own special qualities. If there is time, you may consider letting them take their papers back to their desks and draw on their designs some more.

Alternate Activity

ON ANOTHER piece of paper, you can also have them draw only one doodle and turn it into something from their imagination. You will be surprised what they come up with! Have them add as much detail to this as they want. Even color it if time allows.

These activity cards were originally created by Rich Davis as an art activity for students in public schools and workshops. While working with Angela Hamblen and her staff, the activity cards were shown to them by Rich Davis in the process of brainstorming ideas to help grieving clients. What Angela shares in the beginning of this chapter is what their staff found effective to visually communicate an important concept that they wanted their clients to understand. Angela Hamblen's bio can be viewed on page 99.

Good for the soul

Using Pick and Draw in Grief Counseling with Children

overview

GRIEVING CHILDREN often have a difficult time putting their feelings into words. Younger children don't have the language skills to verbalize intense feelings. They struggle to talk about their loved one's death—the hows, whys, etc.

Grief impacts the entire body and mind and can often be overwhelming for children to process. No child wants to be different. Grieving children immediately feel different not only because they have lost a person out of their life but also because they have feelings that are uncontrollable at times. Pick and Draw provides grieving children a safe outlet to create characters who look different and who experience different emotions. Through the Pick and Draw characters, children experience a safe and fun way to create "people" and then tell the story of why the characters are coming to grief counseling.

Background

AS A LICENSED clinical social worker who has worked in the area of grief counseling for over 10 years, I know that the intensity of grief is often overwhelming to children. This may be the first time they are experiencing feelings at this level of intensity, and they are often afraid of their feelings and afraid that they might never feel normal again. Pick and Draw is a way to take the pressure off the child to tell their story, and it allows them to express their feelings, thoughts and fears through a character they have created.

Getting Started

MATERIALS LIST:

Pick and Draw game,
writing paper/construction paper,
markers

Instructions

USING THE Pick and Draw cards, follow the directions to draw faces. Create three to five characters. After they've drawn several characters, have the child name one character. Then have the child create a story about why that character has come in for counseling. You can also have the child draw a family of characters, then name them and tell a story about a family that is going to grief counseling. I use this activity most often on the child's first grief counseling session.

Discussion

 As you listen to the child's story, pay attention to the following:

1. Who died?

2. How did they die?

3. How does the character feel about being in grief counseling?

4. What does the character say about the person who has died?

5. What does the character miss about the person who died?

 If the child is telling a story about a family, pay attention to answers to these questions:

1. How are the family members feeling?

2. How are the family members interacting with each other?

3. How are the family members expressing or not expressing their grief?

4. What are the family members feeling about being in grief counseling?

Allow the child to tell you the story of the character. Don't assume that the story is a direct illustration of the artist's grief. After the child tells you the story, ask questions to see if the child can tell more of the character's story. At the end, ask if this character and the artist have anything in common? Loss? Feelings? Memories?

Discuss the fact that everyone grieves differently. Just like the characters all look different, grief causes people to feel differently. Share with them that grief is a journey and that it is not a journey to travel alone.

ANGELA HAMBLEN, L.C.S.W., is the Director for the Kemmons Wilson Family Center for Good Grief which is a part of Baptist Trinity Hospice. Angela is a licensed clinical social worker trained specifically in the field of death and dying. Angela received her Certification in Thanatology from ADEC in 2007.

Angela oversees the social services department for three hospice departments for Baptist Trinity Hospice as well as the Center for Good Grief. She directs the three Camp Good Grief programs offered to children, teens and adults who are grieving the loss of a loved one. After the tragedy of September 11, Angela served as a consultant to Schneider Children's Hospital in Long Island, NY, where a program modeled after Camp Good Grief was developed.

She is a recipient of several community awards, including Top 40 Under 40, Health Care Hero Finalist, An Angel in Our Midst, and 50 Women Who Make A Difference. For more information about the Kemmons Wilson Family Center for Good Grief, go to www.baptistonline.org.

*For more helpful
activities, see PAD
Resources on page 135.*

Pick and Draw flexible Drawings for Students with Autism and Related Disorders

overview

ONE CORE characteristic of individuals on the autism spectrum is a deficit in flexible thinking. They have difficulty understanding that things can change on the surface but still be essentially the same. They tend to have rigid, black-and-white thinking and struggle when things vary from what they are used to. This deficit in flexible thinking is part of the complex information processing deficits caused by disordered neurological connectivity.

While the underlying issues that cause rigid and inflexible thinking are complicated, simple strategies can help students with autism to develop more flexible thinking.

The Pick and Draw game provides avenues for students with autism to feel more competent with their drawing and to practice flexible thinking skills. Starting with the simple process of adding features to make a complete face can lead to variations that stretch the student's ability to think flexibly. Each small change in the activity helps the student perceive similarities and differences in safe and meaningful ways.

Background

STUDENTS ON the autism spectrum vary in their level of cognitive functioning, communication abilities, fine motor skills and other areas of functioning. These ideas can be adapted to work for specific students, regardless of their functioning level. While some students may need more support than others, each activity can be implemented to support the development of flexible thinking, social skills, communication and fine motor development.

Start by selecting an appropriate environment that is free from distractions and provides space to work together. A table with two chairs can work well, but some students work better lying on the floor or standing at a counter or other surface. It is also important to select appropriate drawing materials for each student; considering issues such as the thickness and length of writing implements, washability of materials, etc.

To help the student focus on the cards you are working with, remove extra cards from the area. Work with just one card at a time, or have a few of the features out at once. As always, be aware of and adapt to the functioning level of the student. For students who struggle with fine motor skills and do not feel competent at drawing, start with cards that have simpler designs. If needed, allow reluctant students to trace the images on the cards until they build confidence.

Getting Started

MATERIAL LIST:

Pick and Draw cards

pens, pencils, markers, crayons,
or other drawing materials

paper (various colors and sizes)

Instructions

LET THE STUDENT know you will be drawing faces together and show some of the different cards to give an idea of how they look. You can comment on the different types of features and designs on the cards. It may be helpful to show a couple of finished drawings to give an idea of how the images on the cards come together to form complete images. You may also want to demonstrate drawing a face with the cards while the student observes.

Give the student a piece of paper and a writing implement or provide various implements to choose from. You will also have a piece of paper and writing implements. Lay a face card on the table and instruct the student to draw the shape on the paper. You will do the same on your paper. Then lay out the remaining feature cards one at a time, with you and the student drawing each as they are presented. Once the faces are complete, you can comment on how they look the same, how they look different, etc. The focus should be on the process and not on the precision of the drawings. You want to help the student feel competent and successful with the process of making these drawings together!

Once you and the student have experienced success with making faces using various feature cards, you can begin making variations to the activity in order to encourage flexible thinking. Here is a list of variations to get you started:

 Change the order of the feature cards each time you draw a face. This is a small change, but it promotes flexibility with the order things are presented and drawn.

 Separate the feature cards into piles by category and turn then upside down. Take turns flipping over one card from each pile to make the drawing. This adds an element of surprise and also promotes turn taking.

 Each person can select feature cards for the other person to draw.

 Use one piece of paper and draw a face together. You can take turns adding a feature to the drawing so you end up with a collaborative face.

 Name your characters when you are done drawing them. You can also come up with a list of possible names and then collaborate on choosing the best one for each face.

 Make faces with a variety of numbers of features. For example, you can draw a face with two sets of eyes, three noses, etc.

 Add bodies or other elements to the faces to expand them.

Make your own cards with features that are different from the ones in the deck. You can add these to the mix for additional feature options. Use a wide variety of papers and writing implements each time you play the game. Experiment with using different colors, textures and sizes of papers. Try using paints, markers, crayons, pens, pencils and anything else you can think of. For a challenge you can use toothpicks and tin foil to make etchings of the faces!

 Increase the number of people drawing together by adding additional students or adults to the mix.

 Use the same set of five feature cards to make faces of different sizes. Experiment with how big or how small you can make the faces look.

Come up with your own ideas for making all kinds of big and small changes to the game as you go along. Remember to keep the focus on building competence and success and having fun making changes together!

NICOLE BEURKENS, Ph.D. is the founder and director of Horizons Developmental Resource Center in Caledonia, Michigan. She is a licensed psychologist with a doctorate in clinical psychology and a master's degree in special education. She holds a professional teaching certificate with endorsements in autism and learning disabilities and has been certified in many specialized therapies for autism and other neurodevelopmental disorders. Nicole has authored numerous articles and books and writes a popular newsletter for thousands of subscribers each week. With a background in child development, classroom teaching and family-based therapy, Nicole is an award-winning therapist, consultant and speaker for families and school professionals throughout the United States and abroad. You can find more of her strategies for parents and professionals, and sign up to receive her free newsletter at www.HorizonsDRC.com.

Eleven Pick and Draw Heart Messages

For Sunday school; mission trip activities with children; Vacation Bible School; neighborhood children's outreach; youth group meetings; family church festivals and icebreakers for adult meetings

overview

KIDS (AND ADULTS) will understand the message of a sermon longer when they create the visuals themselves. Studies show that doodling boosts memory by almost 30 percent. Pick and Draw provides a fun, relational experience between the leader and the kids while teaching vital heart messages from God's Word, the Bible.

Background

A FUN, HANDS-ON game that promotes visual creative expression is a very powerful tool God has given man to communicate and learn His kingdom truths. Jesus used pictures to communicate His Father's truths through parables. Through His use of simple, uncomplicated visual illustrations, people can grasp His eternal truths in a greater way.

Laughter and enjoyment make up another powerful part of a group learning together. When we laugh (not "at" someone), we are relaxed. And when we are relaxed, it seems we are at the best place to be open and learn. As we follow His lead, using these timeless, biblical heart messages, and pray for His Spirit's moving within those who participate, I believe God will bring blessing on everyone there.

Getting Started

MATERIALS LIST:

Pick and Draw game,

pencil with eraser,

3 pieces of white copier paper,

tape to hang pictures on wall (optional)

Tips that may help with any of these messages:

❤ Play a round of Pick and Draw with the whole group using the same five cards. (See the easy white instruction cards with the deck.)

❤ Tell the group the heart message you want them to get after they've drawn the face. Say it straightforward and repeat it as often as you can. Get the group to repeat it with you if possible. Keep it fun, and keep it moving.

❤ Emphasize the part of the game that visually illustrates the heart message. Example: For Heart Message 3, emphasize that leaving the eyes out makes the face look incomplete. Each of us is part of a group, and not being there makes it incomplete. We are all needed.

❤ Play another hand (draw another face together) and reinforce the heart message again.

♡ Take them to a Scripture that will emphasize the core of the heart message.

♡ Read it aloud and discuss it. (Have them lay their pencils down to cut down on distraction.)

♡ Use simple questions to help them talk about the heart message. Make it applicable to their world, their age and their lifestyle.

♡ Everyone needs encouragement, and a little goes a long way. Be generous with it even if you don't care for what they've done. While learning, a "shared experience" is the goal, not great art.

♡ Allow the kids to hold up their picture and tell about their character if they want to. Use this as a way to teach respecting others by listening attentively when others are sharing. It will also teach them patience in waiting for their turn.

Important: If students name their character each time they draw a face, it will give them a greater sense of ownership. They can also write down something their character loves or is good at.

PICK AND DRAW

EXTRA FUN ACTIVITIES:

♡ ADD A SPEECH BUBBLE out to the side of a character's mouth and write the heart message inside it.

♡ Turn one of your walls into a gallery and let the kids proudly hang up their favorite drawing. Parents will love seeing them and learn the message too!

♡ Let the kids act out what their character's voice would sound like and what it would say.

♡ If it is an older age group doing these activities, you could have fun background music that is upbeat so that it has a fun feeling.

♥ Heart Message 1 ♥

God is the artist who made you.

The Creative Activity: Everyone draws a face using the same five cards that you hold up one by one. Emphasize that they are the artist who created their character the same way that God is the artist who created them.

Scripture possibilities:

Psalm 139:13-16

Isaiah 43:4, 7

1 Cor. 6:20

Discussion starters:

♡ Does God ever mess up when He makes things?

♡ The Mona Lisa painting is valuable because of who painted it. Are you valuable because of how you look and what you can do or because of Who made you?

♡ God the artist is continually creating each day through nature. What is your favorite time of day?

♥ Heart Message 2 ♥

You have been chosen by God for His glory.

The Creative Activity: Instead of you choosing the five cards that the group will use for their cartoon face, fan out the cards face down and let each person choose their own five cards. Then have them draw a cartoon face using those five cards. Emphasize that they got to choose the cards that they used with a purpose in mind.

Note: Pick and Draw can accommodate nine people at the same time. If you have a larger group, either repeat selections a couple of times or use more Pick and Draw games.

Scripture possibilities:

Ephesians 1:4, 5

1 Peter 2:9

Discussion starters:

♡ We all like choices. How does it make you feel knowing that your Creator has chosen you?

♡ Do you have any ideas how He might use you for His glory? Being chosen for something means that God has a plan for something to happen.

♡ What plan do you think God has for man?

♥ Heart Message 3 ♥

You are part of a bigger picture God is making. Your part in His picture is needed and important.

The Creative Activity: You secretly choose only four cards to draw a face, leaving out the eye card, but don't tell the group. Let them take the face drawing all the way to the end and ask them to show them to you. Act surprised and play along to add to the effect of the message. When one of the kids points out that you forgot the eye card, state the heart message. Ask why the face looks weird when a part of it is missing. Emphasize that all parts are needed and work together to make it whole.

Last, be sure to fan the eye cards out and let someone pick the card that everyone will use to add the missing eyes to their picture. Ask them how it looks now.

If you do this again, let them choose which card will be left out, and draw it from the four chosen.

Scripture possibilities:

1 Cor. 12:12, 14, 18
Eph. 4:16

Discussion starters:

♡ What does it feel like when a game or puzzle is missing a piece?

♡ Have you ever thought that God has put you in groups to fulfill His good plan and that you are needed to make that happen?

♡ What groups are you a part of? (family, church, youth group, sports team, workers, etc.)

♥ Heart Message 4 ♥

A desire to create comes from part of God's life in you.

The Creative Activity: Being creative means experimenting and trying new ways that you haven't tried before. It may mean going outside of how you normally think and do things. Ask everyone to fold their paper in half, folding down the tall, vertical end to meet the other end. Now open it back up and smooth out the fold so that it is in the middle of the paper turned sideways. This is like having two pieces of paper to draw on, side by side.

Everyone will draw two cartoon faces at the same time using the same five cards, but try to make them look very different by varying how big they make parts of the face or how far apart things are or how much hair they have, etc. Encourage students to "be creative!"

Fan out the cards and let different people choose 'til you have a set of the five cards needed to draw a face. Then hold them up one at a time as everyone draws two faces.

Scripture possibilities:

Genesis 1:26
Eph. 2:10

Discussion starters:

♡ How did you like drawing two faces differently at the same time?

♡ Was it hard to make them different?

♡ God made us in His image so that we could enjoy creating like He does. Do you think of yourself as creative?

♡ How could you be creative at home that would make others smile?

Ha Ha Ha He He He Ho Ho Ho

POP!

♥ Heart Message 5 ♥

Laughter is a gift from God to man.

The Creative Activity: God gave laughter as a gift to man to help break down walls between us and keep us from taking ourselves too seriously. Laughter can take us through difficult places and cause us to bear hard things well. Use the Pick and Draw instructions on the white cards, but tell your group that they will be creating a sci-fi or alien character of their own design. It's a time where they can put as many eyes or noses or mouths on their character as they want to complete their look. Encourage them to give it a body as well with multiple arms and legs. Name the character, identify the star that it is from, and give the alien a superpower that has to do with laughter. Perhaps, the alien can shoot laughter bombs at people and make them fall over laughing. If possible, draw the superpower in action.

Scripture possibilities:

Proverbs 15:13

Proverbs 17:22

Discussion starters:

♡ What is something funny that happened to you?

♡ Do you think God has a sense of humor?

♡ What do you think God laughs at?

♥ Heart Message 6 ♥

God is writing a story with my life.

The Creative Activity: When a student creates a cartoon character and names it, s/he has created a character that can be featured in a story. Somewhere on the drawing, ask students to write three things about their character: something s/he loves, something s/he's scared of and his/her favorite song.

Turn the paper over and ask students to write something unexpected that happened to their character when s/he went on a mission trip. Encourage them to try and use the things that they wrote about—what the character loves and what s/he was scared of. Give them five to ten minutes depending on the age group. If you have time, let them share them out loud if they want to.

Scripture possibilities:

Psalm 139:16

Rom. 12:1, 2

Discussion starters:

♡ What is your favorite story in the Bible?

♡ What makes it a good story?

♡ Have you thought about giving your whole life to God and asking Him to write your story from now on?

♥ Heart Message 7 ♥

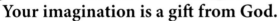

Your imagination is a gift from God.

The Creative Activity: Imagine life without an imagination! God has wired humans to think in pictures to remember, problem solve, create ideas and experience joy. Begin with the usual cartoon face drawing on a full-size sheet of paper. Then instruct students to draw a small body onto their

character, giving him/her clothes they think are funny. Ask the group to brainstorm ideas with you (out loud) where their character could be in the picture. New York? The ocean? Walmart? Their front yard? Church? The moon? Last, let students choose one and draw it in the background around their character.

EXTRA: Draw something in your character's hand that s/he might find useful in this setting.

Scripture possibilities:

Heb. 11:1

Rom. 12:1, 2

Discussion starters:

- How did you think of the place your character would be?

- Why do you think God gave us an imagination for our everyday life?

- How could you use your imagination to pray?

- Do you think the imagination can be tied with faith in some way?

- Can you imagine yourself one day walking into Heaven and seeing Jesus smile at you?

Heart Message 8

Don't be afraid to try.

The Creative Activity: Challenge the group to draw two to four faces at the same time using only the five cards chosen by you or by them. If you draw four, have them fold their paper twice (horizontal, then vertical), then open it up and smooth out the folds. This will give them four equal areas to draw the faces. In order to make the faces different using the same cards, they will have to experiment with making the features bigger or smaller or by placing a feature in different places on the face shape.

This forces student to experiment and take chances. Fear of failing is a tool our enemy uses to try and keep us from growing and reaching dreams God puts in our heart. Talk about fear and faith.

Scripture possibilities:

2 Tim. 1:7

Heb. 13:6

1 Jn. 4:18

Discussion starters:

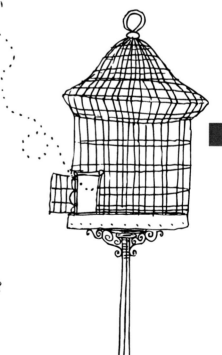

- ♡ How do you feel when you are afraid? Do you like it?

- ♡ Why do you think God doesn't want us to be afraid?

- ♡ What kind of help does God offer us to battle fear inside us?

121

♥ Heart Message 9 ♥

God desires that we enjoy Him and each other.

The Creative Activity: Lay all of the cards out face up so that everyone can see and reach them. Keep each card type (eyes, nose, mouth, etc.) together. Let everyone fish through the cards and select which cards they want to use to make a face. If time allows, let them make several faces this way. Help them work together, sharing cards and communicating. As they create a face, have them name the character and write something funny about it. This activity involves a lot of talking and interaction, which is what you want.

Scripture possibilities:

Mark 12:30, 31

Psalm 37:4

Acts 2:44-47

Discussion starters:

♥ Did you enjoy getting to see what cards you were choosing beforehand?

♥ What is something you really enjoy doing with others?

♥ Why do you think God enjoys spending time with you? Even when you sin?

♥ How could you enjoy God even though you can't see Him?

♥ Heart Message 10 ♥

God's plan for you is full of good surprises.

The Creative Activity: This activity needs to key in on surprises, something that happens that you didn't expect. Instead of the leader choosing the five cards, fan out the cards face down, and let a different person choose each feature. When cards are chosen from the deck, at first kids may experience disappointment. But as they put them into a face, often each person ends up being surprised by the result in a good way.

Scripture possibilities:

Rom. 8:28

Psalm 139:1-6

Discussion starters:

- ♥ Were you surprised with what cards made up your character's face?
- ♥ Were you surprised by anything that happened to you this past week/month?
- ♥ Do you think God can even use bad surprises in a good way if we trust Him?
- ♥ Is God ever surprised?

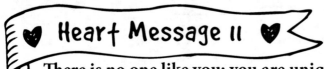

♥ Heart Message 11 ♥

There is no one like you; you are unique!

The Creative Activity: This activity is intended to show that each person's creative expression is unique even though everyone used the same five cards as a prompt for their face drawing. Using the standard directions, create a face and name it. Encourage students to add other things to their character's face to make it funnier: freckles, a hat, glasses, mustache, moles, scars, etc. Display the faces and notice the differences and the humor made by each person. Each face will be unique.

Scripture possibilities:

Psalm 139:13-16

Col. 1:16

Discussion starters:

♥ What does the word "unique" mean? Is that a good thing?

♥ Does making something unique make it more valuable? Why?

♥ Why do you think God made you unique from everyone else?

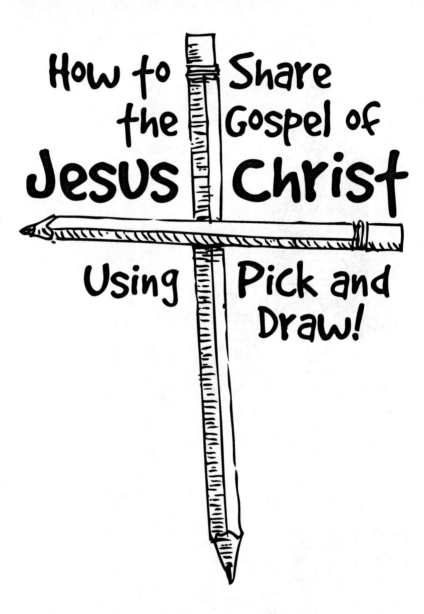

How to Share the Gospel of Jesus Christ Using Pick and Draw!

All sentences in bold are action prompts for the person presenting the Gospel. You can view a demonstration of this by Rich Davis at **pickanddraw.com** by clicking on the icon that says, "Gospel sharing with Pick and Draw."

Begin talk: I want to draw a cartoon face for you today using my Pick and Draw game. As I'm drawing it, I will be telling you about the best news that there is. At the end I'll ask you something very important. I hope you will listen really well.

In the beginning, when I draw a cartoon face, I begin with a big shape that I see on this first card.

Choose the RED card. Show it to your audience. Draw that shape in the middle of the paper. Draw large so everyone can easily see it.

Face

In the beginning, when God was creating everything in Heaven and on earth, His most prized creation was man and woman. The Bible says that He made them in His own image. He also made a beautiful garden for them to call home. God said they could eat fruit from any of the trees in the garden—except one—the tree of the knowledge of good and evil. God told them if they ate the fruit from that tree they would surely die (Genesis 2:17). They were happy and perfect with God in the beginning. There was no sin at all. But Adam and Eve chose to disobey God and eat the fruit. When they disobeyed God, that was called "sin." And sin separated man from God. God is holy and without sin. Adam and Eve had made a very bad choice.

127

Choose the GREEN card. Show it to your audience. DRAW the nose on the inside of the face large.

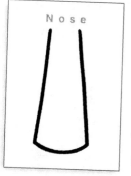

I'm going to give my cartoon face a BIG nose. We use our nose to smell. Sin is like smelly garbage—IT STINKS! Sin is in everyone's heart. (Romans 3:23). That means yours and mine too. Wrong things we have done or said or thought are called sin. The Bible also says that when we sin, we too will die (Romans 6:23). Not only that, but God also says that every person will die once but after that comes the judgment (Hebrews 9:27). Each of us will stand before God, who is without sin, and He will judge us. Any person who has NOT had their sins forgiven and taken away will be punished forever in a very bad place called Hell. We need our sin forgiven and taken away.

Choose a PURPLE card. Show it to your audience. To begin, add only one of the eyes to the face.

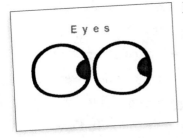

Every cartoon face needs eyes. The first eye that I draw will stand for how all of us see our sin problem. Because of what God has told us in the Bible, we know we are in trouble, and we want to try and do something to change it. We might try to be good and do nice things for others to get God to let us into Heaven. But that doesn't forgive our sin. Our sin is still there, and it stinks

(point to the nose) ! No matter what we try, we can't get rid of our sin! The Bible says that our heart is sinful above all things and really bad (Jeremiah 17:9). You see, it's our heart that needs to be changed.

Draw the second eye on the face.

The second eye I draw will stand for how God sees our need for help. God doesn't want ANYONE to be punished forever in Hell (2 Pet. 3:9). Since He loves us so much, He made a way for all of us to have our sins forgiven and to live with HIM forever.

Choose an ORANGE card. Show it to your audience slowly draw the hair on the head and shade it as you continue talking.

Just like this hair is going to cover my cartoon character's head, God has a way to cover our sins so that they will be forgiven. God's way is the only way we can be saved. His way is through His only Son, Jesus Christ. God had Him die for us on the cross (Romans 5:8). Jesus is the Son of God! He is God's answer for everyone!

Remember, we are the ones who have sinned and done wrong, we deserve to be punished forever. But Jesus came and died in our place on the cross (Rom. 6:23). The cross was how they killed Him. He suffered for us a lot (Isa. 53:5). He did it because He loves us. The Bible tells us that whoever will believe in Jesus as their Savior will not die but will live forever (John 3:16). God gave us no other way that we can have our sins forgiven and live forever except through Jesus Christ (John 14:6). After Jesus died on the cross, they buried His body in a tomb. He was really dead. But on the third day after that, Jesus rose from the dead! This meant that He defeated death for us. He's alive forever! This is the good news of Jesus Christ for all people everywhere (1 Cor. 15:3, 4)! We get to tell others so they can have the chance to live forever too!

Draw the ears. (refer to picture)

Jesus said that if we HEAR His word

Write "HEAR" above the left ear.

…and we BELIEVE in God…

Write "BELIEVE" beside the other ear.

…not only will we have eternal life but God will NOT send us to Hell. We will actually pass from death into life (John 5:24). That means that you only need to believe that Jesus is the Son of God, that He died for your sins, that He was buried, and that He rose again from the dead for you. You've just heard His words.

Point to "HEAR."

The Bible says that your heart is like a room with a door. Jesus stands outside and knocks on the door, asking if you will let Him come in and live with you (Revelations 3:20).

Remember, He's alive forever. He's knocking on the door of your heart right now. Would you be willing to believe in Him so your sins will be forgiven and you'll get to live with Jesus forever in Heaven? If you will, then let's talk to God.

Choose a BLUE card and draw it on the face.

This is a talking mouth. When you pray, you are just talking to God. He hears you. You might want to tell Jesus that you want Him to forgive your sins, come into your heart to live there and give you eternal life. It is a free gift He is wanting to give you. But you have to receive it from Him. God says that if you will receive Jesus into your heart, He will call you His son or daughter. (John 1:12). Will you pray with your mouth so He will do this for you? "Jesus, I believe that You are God's Son and that You died for my sins. I know I am a sinner, and I ask You to forgive all my sins. I open the door of my heart and ask You to come in and live with me forever. Thank You for what You've done for me! Amen."

Mouth

The Bible says that because you called on the name of the Lord to save you, He has now done that (Acts 2:21). God has given you a new, clean heart; your sins are forgiven, and you will live forever with Him!

see follow-up suggestions ➜

Ask those in the group if anyone prayed. If so, ask them to raise their hand. By doing this, they will take the first step toward acknowledging Jesus Christ in front of people.

I suggest having them memorize John 5:24 right away. This verse is an assurance-of-salvation verse that will help them when the enemy later tries to make them doubt that they have eternal life.

Then meet with them later in the week and start them in the book of John to read a chapter each week. Meet and talk about the chapter. Also, coach them on how they can pray on their own (confession, thanksgiving, praying for others, praying for their own needs, and praise). Finally, encourage them to begin sharing Jesus with others whom they know. These things done consistently will give them a solid foundation to continue growing so they can bear good fruit for the rest of their lives.

Yipee!
Jesus Lives in my Heart!!

A personal word from Rich regarding sharing the Gospel:

PRAY BEFORE YOU SPEAK. Only God sees the heart of the person you are talking to. They may appear to be a Christian but are not. They will need to hear from you so that they have every chance to make that eternal choice to follow Jesus and love Him.

It's always best to memorize the verses that God has given us to explain the good news of Jesus Christ. For others' sake, be prepared and know the verse references in case they ask where it is.

Practice. Practice. Practice. It will build confidence in you to share with strangers.

You are not locked in to these exact words. I'm merely showing you how I share it. I have adapted parts of this from the Navigator's Bridge tract. Rely on the Holy Spirit to give you the words you need with your own expression so that it can flow out.

Stay in the Scriptures as you speak because the Bible tells us that they are the power unto salvation (Rom. 1:16). They are powerful because they have come from God (2 Tim. 3:16, 17). When we share, we are speaking with His authority, not our own.

I pray the Lord will give you good fruit from sharing this with others!

October 2012

Resources

Pick and Draw BINGO:

A new spin on a classic game!

MAMA JENN, a Christian wife and homeschooling mom of five children, let her creative juices flow by taking PAD and adapting it to the classic game, Bingo. This is a very fun way to get the whole family involved and enjoy being creative together. We have created a fun PAD Bingo page that you can easily print out and use as often as you like. You can see photos of it being used and download it for your family at: www.mamajennblogs.com/2011/12/pick-and-draw-bingo.html

Thank you, Mama Jenn, for a great idea!

Doodle Activity cards

(pgs. 90-93)

www.richdavis.freewebspace.com/box_widget.html

YOU CAN DOWNLOAD these fun doodle activity cards in two different sizes. The smaller size has four different doodles per piece of letter-size paper. This size is handy for small groups. The larger size has one doodle per piece of letter-size paper. This size is helpful when you have a large group in a big room. Print off as many as you like.

I'd love to hear from you if you enjoyed these at pickanddraw1@yahoo.com.

Autism Spectrum Pick and Draw Helps

SEVERAL BLOGGING MOMS who have children with Autism Spectrum have written reviews for PAD. These reviews have many insightful, hands-on activities that they found effective to help their kids. You may view these at

Not New To Autism
www.notnewtoautism.blogspot.com/2011/01/pick-and-draw-game-and-giveaway.html

Many Hats Mama
www.manyhatsmommy.com/2011/04/24/family-fun-pick-draw/

My Two Happy Homeschoolers
www.mytwohappyhomeschoolers.blogspot.com/2011/03/blessing-in-my-day.html

Sharing the Gospel of Jesus Christ with Pick and Draw
(demo video)

RICH DAVIS takes you through an informal viewing at his drawing table. You can view this at www.pickanddraw.com.

Draw with Rich

MY DRAWING BLOG for kids has many different cartoons to draw step by step and video demos to watch.

www.richdavis1.wordpress.com
http://richdavis1.wordpress.com

Creating Illustrations for a Children's Book

I CHRONICLED MY year-long creative journey when making the children's book *Tiny the Birthday Dog* (Penguin Group) in 2012. This goes from the beginning visual ideas through the completion of the paintings. You may view this at:

www/creatingtinybook.blogspot.com http://creatingtinybook.blogspot.com/

Rich Davis' School and Library Presentations

RICH TRAVELS to many schools and libraries each year to draw with kids and teach them how to develop their creativity. This presentation is a fun drawing time with Rich and will set up teachers to easily take their kids into creative writing exercises. Rich's presentations are for all ages and can accommodate large groups. You may read more about this at:

www.richatyourschool.wordpress.com/ http://richatyourschool.wordpress.com

Contact Rich Davis at
pickanddraw1@yahoo.com

A heartfelt thank you for those who
helped to make this book a reality!

These great folks are Darcy Pattison, Lorinda Gray,
Elizabeth Granderson and Mark Bemenderfer.
God bless you all!

RD

Don't Forget
to exercise
your pencil!

CPSIA information can be obtained at www.ICGtesting.com
Printed in the USA
BVOW03s0049200214

345313BV00014B/236/P

9 780988 351004